SHOOTING FROM THE LIP

SHOOTING FROM THE LIP

Second Edition

HOCKEY'S BEST QUOTES AND QUIPS

Compiled by
CHRIS McDONELL

400 Quotes!

FIREFLY BOOKS

A FIREFLY BOOK

Published by Firefly Books Ltd. 2014

First printing

PUBLISHER CATALOGING-IN-PUBLICATION DATA (U.S.)

A CIP record for this title is available from the Library of Congress.

LIBRARY AND ARCHIVES CANADA CATALOGUING IN PUBLICATION

CIP record for this title is available from Library and Archives Canada.

Published in the United States by
Firefly Books (U.S.) Inc.
P.O. Box 1338, Ellicott Station
Buffalo, New York 14205

Published in Canada by
Firefly Books Ltd.
50 Staples Avenue, Unit 1
Richmond Hill, Ontario L4B 0A7

Cover and interior design by Ingrid Paulson
Printed in China

The publisher gratefully acknowledges the financial support for our publishing program by the Government of Canada through the Canada Book Fund as administered by the Department of Canadian Heritage.

To Quinn, Tara and Isaac McDonell-Gordon
and Sue Gordon, for their patience,
love and understanding

CONTENTS

INTRODUCTION

"It would have been worse if we hadn't blocked the kick after Toronto's second touchdown," quipped Detroit captain Alex Delvecchio on January 2, 1971. His team had just endured an embarrassing 13–0 shellacking by the Toronto Maple Leafs. In the midst of one of the Motor City franchise's bleakest seasons, Delvecchio's wisecrack showed the resiliency that helped him to a 24-season Hall of Fame career. He also used wit to put perspective on a hockey disaster, sending a message to his teammates and to their fans. More than thirty years later, Wayne Gretzky, the managing partner of the Phoenix Coyotes, tried to give his struggling team similar advice: "It's time for them to stop feeling sorry for themselves, and time to go out and play. You play hard, you'll enjoy it. If you enjoy it, you're winning." The National Hockey League is a billion-dollar business, but the secret of success in hockey, even at its highest level, is to treat it like a game. This book takes that advice to heart.

Shooting From the Lip is full of the off-the-cuff comments that keep millions of fans not only watching the games, but also tuning in to see the highlight reels and reading the sports pages religiously. Most of these lines have burst out of the rumble and tumble of the daily grind, from the post-game scrum, the between-periods interview, or over a beer with an attentive scribe. They're fresh, they're frank, and they're all about hockey.

There are serious and earnest comments that bear repeating for their pithy accuracy and insight. Sarcasm, insult and downright trash talking also abound, for the tough, mean and nasty side of the game is as integral to the NHL as its grace and beauty. But colorful tributes and sincere praise are in the mix, too. Just as we all like to see the vain, greedy and lazy get their comeuppance, so too do we enjoy seeing the talented, dedicated and worthy get their due. Hockey players, coaches and management are no different, and the evidence is here.

Is there any athlete more self-deprecating than an NHL player? "It's nice to get a standing ovation in Montreal," noted Florida Panther Scott Mellanby, his tongue firmly planted in his cheek. Mellanby got his round of applause while leaving the ice on a stretcher after crashing headfirst into the boards. There are plenty of other laughs here too, for humor is the glue that binds this compilation together. Of course, sometimes the funny remark is unintentional. "It's not so much maturity as it is growing up," responded Boston Bruins enforcer Jay Miller, when asked if his improved play could be attributed to maturity. Sorry to Jay and many others, but your verbal gaffes have been recorded for posterity.

There are 400 quotations gathered here, arranged by topic. Speakers are identified by their affiliation at the time the lines were spoken. Unless it is critical to understanding the relevance of the quote, dates have been omitted. Most of these lines are of recent vintage, but some are fifty years old, proving that hockey remains hockey. Goalie Gump Worsley's blunt observation that champagne drunk from the Stanley Cup "tasted like horse pee from a tin cup" is as iconoclastic a comment today as it was in the 1960s. Likewise, Bobby Clarke's admission, "If I hadn't learned to lay on a two hander once in a while, I'd never have left Flin Flon," resonates as strongly with those of us who know him only as the Philadelphia Flyers' general manager in 2004 as it does with those of us who watched him play in the 1970s.

Whether you're a hockey fan who'll dip into these pages for random nibbles or one who'll devour them in one sitting, cover to cover, you'll find plenty here to satisfy any desire. Bon appetit!

"Every boo on the road is a cheer."

WINGS COACH **SCOTTY BOWMAN**

"You're really playing against yourself. You have to learn what you can control and what you can't, and not let what you can't control affect your confidence."

RANGERS GOALIE **MIKE RICHTER**

"You try to block out all the negatives. You worry about all the negatives, you end up in a rubber room."

SHARK **GARY SUTER**

"Great moments are born from great opportunities."

TEAM USA "MIRACLE ON ICE" COACH **HERB BROOKS**

"I think I'm past trying to prove people wrong. I'm just trying to live up to my own expectations. If you're not motivated, you're never going to get to where you want to go."

LIGHTNING **MARTIN ST. LOUIS**, ON BEING QUESTIONED FOR HIS SMALL SIZE

"It's not about what you did yesterday—it's what you do tomorrow. If you rely too much on yesterday, tomorrow is going to jump up and bite you in the pants."

FLYERS GOALIE **JOHN VANBIESBROUCK**, AFTER BEING BENCHED THE PREVIOUS NIGHT

"In the playoffs, will beats skill."

SHARKS COACH **KEVIN CONSTANTINE**

"We're going
to be the best
in the league
at something.
We're deep in
anthem singers."

PREDATORS COACH BARRY TROTZ

"He could deke a guy in a phone booth."

SHARK **OWEN NOLAN**, ON TEAMMATE VIKTOR KOZLOV

"Great lines in hockey could turn the lights off and know where each other is."

COYOTES GM **MIKE BARNETT**, ON COYOTES
TONY AMONTE AND DANNY BRIERE

"How you can have a guy who is [so small] dominate a hockey game like he does? He's mastered the art of being able to just stop and turn on a dime and avoid the monsters who are chasing him."

FLYER **JEREMY ROENICK**, ON PREDATOR CLIFF RONNING,
WHO HAD JUST PLAYED IN HIS 1,000TH NHL GAME

"There is no escalator to success—only steps."

OILERS GM **GLEN SATHER**

"I'm on the third line. I'm a crasher. I know my role. I'm just trying to help. I'm not stupid enough to think I'm great out there."

LEAF **DARCY TUCKER**

"Some of us were meant to score, others were meant to play goal. And others were meant to do what I do. I tick people off and I don't get danger pay."

CANADIEN **TRENT McCLEARY**

"We know he is a one-dimensional player, but it's the dimension we don't have."

FLAMES GM **AL COATES**, ON PHIL HOUSLEY

"I have 3,000 penalty minutes. I don't need people dictating to me how to do my job."

LEAF **TIE DOMI**, ON FAN AND MEDIA CRITICISM

"I'm older."

CANUCK **HENRIK SEDIN,** WHEN ASKED WHY
HE MISSED A PRACTICE THAT HIS TWIN BROTHER
DANIEL SEDIN ATTENDED

"Why would we be interested in acquiring Fedorov? We already have one Fedorov too many."

CANUCKS GM **BRIAN BURKE**, ASKED IF HIS TEAM WAS INTERESTED IN ACQUIRING SERGEI FEDOROV TO PLAY WITH HIS BROTHER FEDOR OF THE CANUCKS

"Pumped I am no longer an unemployed 23-year-old living with his parents."

PREDATOR **COLIN WILSON**, ON HOW HE FELT ABOUT THE END OF THE NHL LOCKOUT

"At the time it happened, I wasn't disappointed, but I came in the dressing room and I was real upset with what happened. That's blood, man.... Right away I came in and called my parents and apologized."

WHALER **KEITH PRIMEAU**, AFTER FIGHTING HIS BROTHER WAYNE OF THE SABRES

"It's a terrible time of year to have a baby. Of course, she got married on draft day, so I think she has no idea what I do for a living."

NHL DIRECTOR OF OFFICIATING **BRYAN LEWIS**, ON HIS DAUGHTER EXPECTING DURING THE PLAYOFFS

"Let's put it this way: if one of my brothers were standing in front of the bus last night and we were about to leave and he was on the other team, I'd have run over him. I wouldn't have called out first to ask him to get out of the way, either. That's my mentality, that's the way it is. I don't really care."

BLACKHAWKS COACH **BRIAN SUTTER**, DURING
A CHICAGO-ST. LOUIS PLAYOFF SERIES

"Ah, my sister used to hit me harder."

WING **SHAWN BURR**, ON BEING CHECKED BY
DALLAS STAR MIKE MODANO

"I'll still run him on the ice tomorrow."

LEAF **TIE DOMI**, AFTER RANGER ADAM GRAVES (RELATED TO
HIM BY MARRIAGE) DROVE HIM TO TORONTO'S PRACTICE IN
RYE, NEW YORK

"We had too many guys hurt their arms patting themselves on the back. Now, they're probably rubbing their feet from being sore kicking themselves."

COYOTES COACH **JIM SCHOENFELD**, AFTER BLOWING
A 4-1 LEAD AND LOSING TO TORONTO

"It would have been worse if we hadn't blocked the kick after Toronto's second touchdown."

WING **ALEX DELVECCHIO**, AFTER TORONTO BEAT DETROIT 13-0 IN 1971

"I'm glad that my sons are too young to count!"

NORDIQUE **STEVEN FINN**, AFTER HIS TEAM'S 10-3 LOSS TO THE CAPITALS IN 1991

"Well, they were the only two I had."

LIGHTNING COACH **TERRY CRISP**, ASKED WHY HE USED HIS TWO GOALIES IN A 10-0 LOSS

"The only difference between this and Custer's last stand was Custer didn't have to look at the tape afterwards."

LIGHTNING COACH **TERRY CRISP**, AFTER A COMPLETELY ONE-SIDED LOSS

"**Man is that guy ripped.
I mean, I've got the
washboard stomach, too.
It's just that mine
has about two months
of laundry on top of it.**"

SHARK **SHAWN BURR**, ON FLYER ERIC LINDROS

"It must be the body. It's chiseled out of marshmallows."

BLACKHAWK **TONY AMONTE**, ON POSSESSING THE
NHL'S SECOND-LONGEST ACTIVE PLAYING STREAK

"Every time I see you naked, I feel sorry for your wife."

PENGUIN **JAROMIR JAGR**, TO TEAMMATE MATTHEW
BARNABY

"They're scared of the beard and the unibrow."

PENGUIN **PASCAL DUPUIS**, ON WHY OPPONENTS
WON'T FIGHT HIM

"If he had another hair on his back, he'd be up a tree."

CANADIEN **KENNY REARDON**, ON TEAMMATE
MAURICE RICHARD

"We don't care what that bug-eyed fat walrus has to say."
CANADIEN **BRANDON PRUST**, ON SENATORS COACH PAUL MACLEAN

"I am not fat. I might be husky, but I am not fat."

SENATORS COACH **PAUL MACLEAN**, IN RESPONSE TO BRANDON PRUST

"They always try to play with our minds. But that won't work with our club. We've got 20 guys without brains."

FLYER **BOBBY CLARKE**, IN 1976, WHEN THE RUSSIAN CENTRAL ARMY TEAM PLAYED PHILADELPHIA

"There's a thousand theories, but theories are for scientists. We're too stupid for that. We've just got to get back to the x's and o's."

SHARK **MIKE RICCI**, ON SAN JOSE'S SLOW START

"I see you finally got a number to match your IQ."

OILERS ASSISTANT COACH **BOB McCAMMON**, TO MARTY McSORLEY, WHO WAS WEARING NO. 5

"I was young and stupid then. Now I'm not young anymore."

LEAF **JYRKI LUMME**, ON HIS EARLY YEARS WITH MONTREAL

"We've given up seven goals in two games and we haven't scored one. They're playing chess and we're playing checkers."

JETS COACH **CLAUDE NOEL**

"You can always get someone to do your thinking for you."

HALL OF FAME RED WING **GORDIE HOWE**, DURING A
1970S APPEARANCE ON "THE DICK CAVETT SHOW,"
ON WHY HOCKEY PLAYERS ALWAYS WEAR A PROTECTIVE
CUP BUT RARELY A HELMET

"I don't know what that word means, but he's weird."

CANADIAN **BRAYDEN SCHENN**, ASKED WHETHER HIS
CANADIAN WORLD JUNIOR ROOMMATE, LOUIS LEBLANC,
WAS ECCENTRIC

"Because there wasn't enough time to play 54."

OILERS GOALTENDER **GRANT FUHR**, AFTER BEING ASKED
HOW HE COULD PLAY 36 HOLES OF GOLF IN THE MIDDLE OF
THE STANLEY CUP FINALS

"I don't know if I think Hullie's funny, but I can tell
you this: He sure thinks he is."

STAR **CRAIG LUDWIG**, ON TEAMMATE BRETT HULL

"He lightens up the room. Sometimes we laugh
when he's not even trying to tell a joke."

CANUCK **KEVIN BIEKSA**, ON TEAMMATE ALEX BURROWS

"Hopefully someone on their team addresses it, because, uh, I'm not saying I'm going to do it, but something might happen to him if he continues to be that cocky."

FLYER **MIKE RICHARDS** ON ROOKIE P.K. SUBBAN'S LACK
OF RESPECT FOR VETERAN PLAYERS

"We've actually been telling Patty to grow up for years. He brings his Legos on the road."

SABRE **JASON POMINVILLE**, ON THE SUSPENSION OF HIS
TEAMMATE PATRICK KALETA

"I'd rather hide what a nut I am than reveal it to the whole world like he does."

BRUINS GOALTENDER **TIM THOMAS**, ON FLYERS' GOALIE ILYA
BRYZGALOV'S STRANGE STAR TURN IN HBO'S 24/7

"You know that creepy-looking guy you stare at two seats behind you, thinking 'who would come to a movie by himself?' That's me."

HALL OF FAME WINGER **BRENDAN SHANAHAN**, ON HOW HE RELAXES AWAY FROM THE RINK

"I've said this before, but it's really true: you have to get players to do what they don't want to do."

FLYERS COACH **KEN HITCHCOCK**

"I know my players don't like my practices, but that's O.K. because I don't like their games."

CANUCKS COACH **HARRY NEALE**

"You can't play hockey if you're nice."

LIGHTNING COACH **STEVE LUDZIK**

"I live in a house with mirrors. So that's the first place I look."

JETS COACH **CLAUDE NOEL**, WHEN ASKED WHERE HE SEARCHES FOR EXPLANATIONS WHEN THINGS ARE GOING BADLY

"**Maybe one of the qualities of being a great**

coach

is being a jerk.

There are quite a few of them around."

KINGS COACH **LARRY ROBINSON**

"Coaches are like ducks. Calm on top but paddling underneath. Believe me, there's a lot of leg movement."

STARS COACH **KEN HITCHCOCK**, ON HIDING HIS NERVOUSNESS

"This is my third time. They say you're not a coach in the league till you've been fired. I must be getting pretty good."

JETS COACH **TERRY SIMPSON**, AFTER BEING FIRED

"Just because you can draw it doesn't mean it can happen."

WING **STEVE YZERMAN**, ON GAME PLANS

"You **can't** keep on trading foot soldiers. Sooner or later, the **general's** got to go."

LEAFS COACH **PAT BURNS**, AFTER BEING FIRED BY TORONTO

"Everybody's diving now. You used to dive and go back to the bench and guys would bitch at you and say: 'Come on. Don't embarrass us.' Now you get a high five."

CANUCKS GM **BRIAN BURKE**

"It was a nose dive, a swan dive, a double gainer. I'm surprised he didn't flip backwards in the air while he was doing it."

PANTHERS COACH **MIKE KEENAN**, ON THE WAY COYOTE DANIEL BRIERE WENT DOWN AFTER BEING HOOKED BY PANTHER OLLI JOKINEN

"He's going down like free beer at a frat party."

BROADCASTER **PIERRE MCGUIRE**, ON ISLANDER MARIUSZ CZERKAWSKI'S FREQUENT DIVING

"My old man used
to tell me,
'If you ain't dead,
don't lay there.'
Maybe a lot of
guys didn't have
fathers telling them
that."

OILERS GM **KEVIN LOWE**, ON PLAYERS
WHO FAKE INJURY TO DRAW A PENALTY

"Mike Richards was yelling—
something to the effect of

'It looks like a
yard sale out here.'

He had gloves thrown all over
the place, he was grabbing his
face, taking dives.
And then he would complain to
the referee that he was **fouled**."

FORMER REFREE **KERRY FRASER**, ON PENGUIN SIDNEY CROSBY'S
BEHAVIOR IN A GAME AGAINST PHILADELPHIA

"It's about 40 percent technique and about 75 percent strength."

SIX-FOOT-ONE CANADIEN **PATRICE BRISEBOIS**, ON WHY HE
LOST A FIGHT TO FIVE-FOOT-SIX FLAME THEO FLEURY

"Our team can't afford to have 5 percent of the guys not playing 100 percent. But when we've got 95 percent not giving 100 percent, we're in real trouble."

KINGS COACH **BOB BERRY**, IN 1980

"I don't know about the percentage, but I'm halfway there."

BLACKHAWK **DAVE BOLLAND**, ON RECOVERING FROM A GROIN PULL

"Are we mathematically eliminated yet?"

SENATOR **JASON SPEZZA**, ATTEMPTING TO CALM OTTAWA FANS AFTER HIS TEAM LOST TWO OF THEIR FIRST THREE GAMES

"I'd say there's 100 percent of the guys who think they're in the 25 percent."

BLUE **DOUG WEIGHT**, RESPONDING TO BRETT HULL'S CLAIM THAT "75 PERCENT OF THE PLAYERS ARE OVERPAID"

"He gets this now. He'll get comfortable with it and next year maybe he can mix in the secret handshake."

CANUCK **KEVIN BIEKSA**, ON LETTING TEAMMATE ALEX EDLER MONITOR THE DRESSING ROOM CLOCK

"I don't know who it is. I don't see these guys naked often enough to know."

CAPITALS ASSISTANT COACH **TIM HUNTER**, ASKED TO IDENTIFY THE NUDE CAPITAL SHOWERING IN THE BACKGROUND DURING PETER BONDRA'S POST-GAME INTERVIEW

"Everything was set for us to play a real good game. Then we left the dressing room and everything went to hell."

THRASHERS COACH **CURT FRASER**

"If you're looking for the guy we got for Marty, he'll be here in four years."

DUCK **STEVE SHIELDS**, BITTER AFTER TEAMMATE MARTY MCINNIS WENT TO BOSTON FOR A DRAFT PICK

The playoffs separate
        the men from the boys,
and we found out
        we have a lot of boys
        in our dressing room.

RANGERS GM **NEIL SMITH**, AFTER THE RANGERS LOST
IN THE PLAYOFFS TO WASHINGTON

**"There's no reason why
a player is done at 33, 34.
They train better,
they eat better,
they drink better.
This isn't the old days
when everybody
sat around
and drank beer."**

FLYERS GM **BOB CLARKE**, ON SIGNING
37-YEAR-OLD KJELL SAMUELSSON

"Usually, I'm on the bus by now, having a beer and waiting for everyone else. This is cutting into my beer time."

CAPITAL **CRAIG BERUBE**, TO THE MEDIA, AFTER SCORING ONE OF HIS RARE GOALS AND BEING THE CENTER OF ATTENTION IN THE DRESSING ROOM

"Bud Light."

BLUE **KEITH TKACHUK**, ASKED TO NAME HIS FAVORITE SPORTS DRINK IN THE TEAM MEDIA GUIDE

"Maybe I'd drink a bit more."

HALL OF FAME NHL AND WHA PLAYER **BOBBY HULL**, WHEN ASKED WHAT HE WOULD DO IF HE HAD TO DO HIS CAREER ALL OVER AGAIN

"The kids just aren't the same today."

CANADIEN **DOUG GILMOUR**, AFTER ASKING A ROOKIE TO SNEAK A CASE OF 24 BEERS ONTO THE TEAM BUS AND FINDING OUT HE ONLY GOT SIX CANS

"Use good fertilizer. Molson Canadian works for me"

SENATORS COACH **PAUL MACLEAN**, ASKED FOR HIS ADVICE ON GROWING A GOOD MOVEMBER MOUSTACHE

"First of all, it's a curse. Voodoo. As soon as a guy gets put on the cover of *The Hockey News*, it's like *Sports Illustrated*. He goes right into the tank."

KINGS GM **DEAN LOMBARDI**, ON KING ANZE KOPITAR, WHOSE PLAY DECLINED AFTER BEING FEATURED ON THE COVER OF A MAGAZINE

"When you only score two, you remember them all."

SABRES ENFORCER **JOHN SCOTT**, AFTER SCORING IN TORONTO, ON WHETHER HE COULD REMEMBER HIS LAST NHL GOAL

"When I was awful, early in the season, it looked like I was shooting at a lacrosse net. Now, it's like a soccer goal!"

CAPITAL **MIKE GARTNER**, AFTER ENDING A 1987 SCORING DROUGHT WITH A FLURRY OF GOALS

"It was so long I thought somebody would have to come up with those paddles and shock me back to life."

PREDATOR **BILL HOULDER**, ON ENDING A 144-GAME SCORING DROUGHT

"Only problem is I was going high on the glove side."

SENATOR **LANCE PITLICK**, ON SCORING HIS FIRST GOAL
OF THE SEASON WITH A LOW SHOT TO THE STICK SIDE

"I like to space them out so I can remember them."

FLYER **CHRIS McALLISTER**, AFTER SCORING
HIS FIRST GOAL IN 94 GAMES

"I'm on fire."

CANUCK **DARREN LANGDON**, AFTER GETTING AN ASSIST
FOR HIS FIRST POINT IN 32 GAMES

"It's not so much maturity as it is growing up."

BRUIN **JAY MILLER**, ASKED IF HIS IMPROVED PLAY
WAS DUE TO MATURITY

"I'll be sad to go and I wouldn't be sad to go. It wouldn't upset me to leave St. Louis, but it would upset me to leave St. Louis. It's hard to explain. You'll find out one of these days, but maybe you never will."

BLUE **BRETT HULL**, ON A POSSIBLE TRADE

"Right now, it's a mid-body. But picking my nose, it's an upper-body."

LEAF **CARL GUNNARSSON**, ON THE DIFFERENCE
BETWEEN UPPER-BODY AND LOWER-BODY INJURIES, AFTER
TAKING A SHOT OFF HIS RING FINGER

"Yeah, I'm cocky and I am arrogant. But that doesn't mean I'm not a nice person."

COYOTE **JEREMY ROENICK**

"Jason Arnott will be here as long as I'm here, for the time being."

OILERS GM **GLEN SATHER**, ON JASON ARNOTT TRADE RUMORS

"The worst thing you can do is **overreact**. But it's also not good to **underreact** either."

DEVILS GM **LOU LAMORIELLO**, AFTER THE DEFENDING STANLEY CUP CHAMPIONS FAILED TO MAKE THE PLAYOFFS

"Guys, I don't want to tell you half-truths, unless they're completely accurate."

CANADIENS COACH **ALAIN VIGNEAULT**, AFTER A LOSS IN 1999

"I told him to get some blood on it—that would be awesome."

WINGS FAN **TERI RODRIGUEZ**, WHO LOANED RED WING TOMAS HOLMSTROM HER REPLICA HOLMSTROM SWEATER WHEN THE DETROIT PLAYER'S JERSEY WENT MISSING JUST BEFORE AN INTRASQUAD GAME

"I had a [Detroit fan] yelling at me on my own bench. I was waiting for a [Phoenix fan] to stand up and do something. I don't want to say, 'Start a fight.' But at least throw some popcorn on the guy."

COYOTE **TODD SIMPSON**, AFTER BEING HECKLED DURING A HOME GAME

"Ranger fans are the rudest and they're proud of it, I'm sure."

BRUIN **BYRON DAFOE**

"They don't know a lick about hockey. They never leave in the third period because they think there's a fourth one."

PREDATOR **TOM FITZGERALD**, ON NASHVILLE FANS

"He could rile up the Montreal fans in a hurry. God, sometimes I felt sorry for the man. He must have got a standing ovation when he went shopping."

HALL OF FAME RED WING **GORDIE HOWE**, ON MAURICE RICHARD

"We're giving the fans their money's worth. We're super-sizing the games for them."

PANTHER **PETER WORRELL**, ON FLORIDA'S 13 OVERTIME GAMES BY MIDWAY THROUGH THE SEASON

"I'm just glad it wasn't Machete Night."

RANGER **BOB FROESE**, AFTER FANS THREW PLASTIC MUGS ONTO THE ICE ON MUG NIGHT

"It's always good to have the building filled, even if it's with low-IQ Rangers fans."

ISLANDERS GM **MIKE MILBURY**, BEFORE A HOME GAME AGAINST THE NEW YORK RANGERS

"People ask me,
'How do you

do it at 38?'

"I don't know what 38 feels like. It's my first time."

LIGHTNING **MARTIN ST. LOUIS**, ON PLAYING IN THE
NHL AT HIS AGE

"I never thought I'd be an old, fat, ex-hockey player, but I became one."

LEAFS GM AND COACH **PAT QUINN**

"If I'd known it was going to take 25 years, I'd have started earlier."

STAR COACH **KEN HITCHCOCK**, ON HOW LONG
IT TOOK HIM TO GET TO THE STANLEY CUP FINALS

"I've smelled enough sweat. After 61 years, I'm going to give it up. I don't want to stay here till I'm 100. That's too long."

WINGS LOCKER ROOM ASSISTANT **WALLY CROSSMAN**, ON
RETIRING AT AGE 91

"No, I don't fight anybody I played against in Juniors. I think everyone I played Juniors with is dead now."

KING **KELLY BUCHBERGER**

"So my decision, after 16 years, was to walk away now, rather than crawl away later."

HALL OF FAME NHL PLAYER **DALE HAWERCHUK**, ON HIS
REASON TO RETIRE

"Sometimes it could be your legs, sometimes it's your hands. I don't think the brain ever goes. You still have those natural instincts about where to go. I hate to tell you, but I think you lose your verve or your enthusiasm for the game. I think that's part of it."

RETIRED NHL PLAYER **PAT VERBEEK**, ON WHEN
IT'S TIME TO HANG UP YOUR SKATES

"I'm convinced the head goes before the body. You end up not wanting to pay the price. It happens to every athlete eventually. In a physical contact sport, it shows up quicker. A guy gets tired of hitting or being hit. You can't hide that once it happens."

NHL PLAYER, COACH AND GM **BOBBY CLARKE**

"I didn't drop my gloves. They were yanked off me."

STAR **MIKE MODANO**, ON HIS 1997 FIGHT WITH OILER KELLY BUCHBERGER

"I had a poster of Probert on my wall. When I fought him for the first and only time, I thought to myself, 'Great, I got out alive.' "

ISLANDER **ERIC CAIRNS**, ON HIS CHILDHOOD IDOL BOB PROBERT

"Broken nose, broken jaw—that's the quickest way to get the point across. There's no sense getting into a fight if you're not trying to hurt them."

FLYER **DAVE BROWN**, ON HIS FIGHTING TACTICS

"Two people fighting is not violence in hockey. It might be in tennis or bowling, but it's not in hockey."

NHL GOALIE AND COACH **GERRY CHEEVERS**

"I don't even like talking about fighting. **It's not an honor.** As a kid, I was always the top scorer on my team. Would I rather have a good fight or a goal? I celebrate every goal like it's my last."

OILER **GEORGES LARAQUE,**
ON BEING VOTED THE NHL'S TOP FIGHTER

"The truth is I would never

spit

on somebody. I would

punch

him first."

WING **MARTIN LAPOINTE,** ON AN ACCUSATION HE, STEVE YZERMAN AND SCOTTY BOWMAN ASSAULTED CAMERAMEN IN TAMPA BAY

"For the most part, with the possible exception of me, I don't think anybody goes out to try to hurt somebody."

FLYER **JEREMY ROENICK**

"I don't bother people unless they bother me. I just try to give myself a little working room. But if a guy bothers me, then I retaliate."

ISLANDERS GOALIE **BILLY SMITH**

"Dirty isn't a derogatory word. It's a good thing to be in hockey."

WING **STEVE YZERMAN**, ASKED ABOUT
CAPITAL DALE HUNTER'S STYLE

"I'm not dirty, just aggressive. Fighter pilots have machine guns. I have only my mask and stick."

BRUINS GOALIE **GERRY CHEEVERS**

"**I play a position where you make mistakes. The only people who don't make them at a hockey game are the ones watching.**"

AVALANCHE GOALIE **PATRICK ROY**

"With goaltenders, when they are on, the pucks look like beach balls. When they are a little bit off, they look like BBs."

PREDATORS COACH **BARRY TROTZ**

"Yeah, the two that went in."

BRUINS GOALIE **GERRY CHEEVERS**, ASKED IF HE COULD REMEMBER ANY SHOTS THAT WERE PARTICULARLY DIFFICULT TO HANDLE IN A 2-2 TIE AGAINST PHILADELPHIA

"The goalie is like the guy on the minefield. He discovers the mines and destroys them. If you make a mistake, somebody gets blown up."

HURRICANES GOALIE **ARTURS IRBE**

"Maybe we should hire another coach, so we can push him."

STARS GOALIE **ED BELFOUR**, AFTER HEARING HIS COACH KEN HITCHCOCK WANTED BACKUP MARTY TURCO TO PUSH HIM FOR THE NUMBER ONE JOB

"How would you like it if, at your job, every time you made the slightest mistake a little red light went on over your head and 18,000 people stood up and screamed at you?"

HALL OF FAME CANADIENS GOALIE **JACQUES PLANTE**

• 69 •

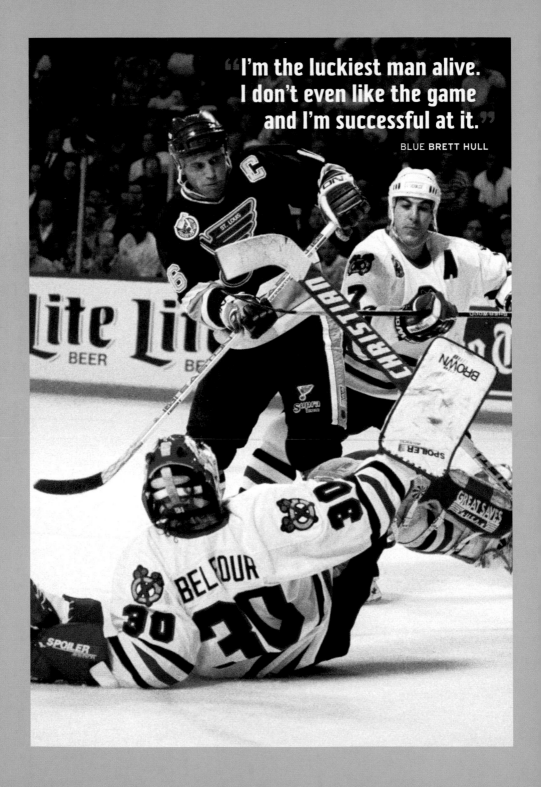

"I'm the luckiest man alive. I don't even like the game and I'm successful at it."

BLUE BRETT HULL

"How's the game changed in my 15 years in the league? Well, we used to be called hard-working players. Now we're overpaid crybabies."

WING **BRETT HULL**

"It's like the animal kingdom. Adapt or go extinct."

WING **BRETT HULL**, ON ADJUSTING HIS STYLE WHILE CONTINUING TO SCORE GOALS

"I am 10 times smarter than everyone else in this game. Beyond a shadow of a doubt."

WING **BRETT HULL**

"Hullie's a lot like a garbage can. You step on the pedal with your foot and the top opens up."

BLUE **WAYNE GRETZKY**, ON TEAMMATE BRETT HULL'S FREQUENTLY CONTROVERSIAL QUOTES

"A.m. or p.m.?"

CANADA'S **STEVE YZERMAN**, RESPONDING TO 1998 TEAM USA OLYMPIAN HULL'S CLAIM THAT "EIGHT NIGHTS OUT OF TEN, I WAS IN BED BY EIGHT."

"Fifty percent of the game is **mental** and the other fifty percent is **being mental.** I've got that part down, no problem."

BLUE **BASIL McRAE**

"I remember my first year, I hit him with three good punches and couldn't believe he was still standing. He hit me with one and cracked my helmet. My head hurt for a week."

OILER **GEORGES LARAQUE**, ON STU GRIMSON

"If I play badly I'll pick a fight in the third, just to get into a fight. I'll break a guy's leg to win, I don't care. Afterward I say, 'Yeah, all right, I played badly, but I won the fight so who gives a damn.'"

BRUIN **DEREK SANDERSON**

"All my friends back home fight on the street, and all they get is arrested."

PREDATOR **PATRICK COTE**, ON HIS $375,000 SALARY, MOSTLY EARNED AS A FIGHTER

"I'd rather fight than score."

FLYER **DAVE "THE HAMMER" SCHULTZ**

"If it keeps going like this, the Zamboni driver is going to be the first star."

DON CHERRY, ON A BORING GAME

"After a year, I got so much to say I can hardly wait to hear myself."

DON CHERRY, AFTER THE 2004–05 NHL LOCKOUT

"How would you like that guy operating on you with those hands?"

DON CHERRY, ON OILER RANDY GREGG, A DOCTOR, MISSING A CHANCE ON A WIDE-OPEN NET

"Here's Wellwood, 7-and-0 in the faceoffs, plus-two, two assists, played 20 minutes, drew eight minutes on the power play, lost a tooth and a pint of blood. What a guy."

DON CHERRY DISCUSSING THE PLAY OF LEAF KYLE WELLWOOD

"I know those guys who wear visors are sweeties, but that's a little too much."

DON CHERRY, ON ISLANDER ZIGMUND PALFFY KISSING TEAMMATE TRAVIS GREEN ON THE LIPS WHILE CELEBRATING A GOAL

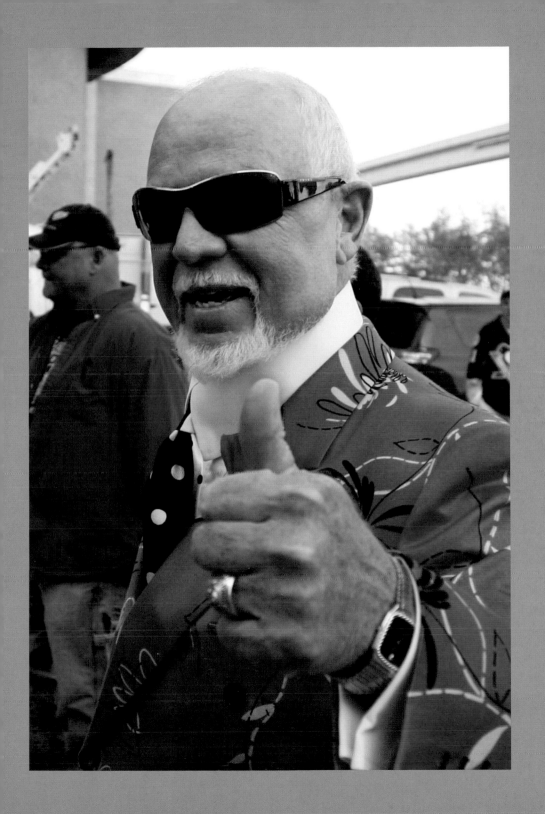

"I can't hear what Jeremy says because I've got my two Stanley Cup rings plugging my ears."

AVALANCHE **PATRICK ROY**, RESPONDING TO A REMARK FROM BLACKHAWK JEREMY ROENICK

"Some nights, I'd like to shoot some of them myself."

RANGERS PRESIDENT **NEIL SMITH**, RESPONDING TO FASHION PHOTOGRAPHER BRUCE WEBER'S STATEMENT THAT HE WOULD LIKE TO SHOOT SOME OF THE RANGERS

"Every time a puck gets past me and I look back in my net, I say 'Oh, oh.'"

FLYERS GOALIE **BERNIE PARENT**, ON WHY HE CHOSE NUMBER 00 IN THE WHA

"Yeah. Several fans."

FLYERS COACH **ROGER NEILSON**, ASKED IF ANYONE
SUGGESTED HE STOP COACHING WHEN HE ANNOUNCED
HE HAD BONE CANCER

"What are you doing in this league?"

CANADIEN **CHRIS NILAN**, TO FLYER ENFORCER DAVE
BROWN, WHO QUESTIONED WHAT NILAN WAS DOING ON
MONTREAL'S POWER PLAY

"I heard Rolex makes nice watches."

CANADIEN **BRENDAN GALLAGHER**, TO NEW TEAMMATE
MICHAEL RYDER UPON GIVING RYDER HIS JERSEY NO. 73

"Sure, Daniel wears number 22 and Henrik number 33."

CANUCKS COACH **MARC CRAWFORD**, ON WHETHER
HE COULD TELL THE SEDIN TWINS APART

"He is definitely reckless and he's not always in control of what's going on. I have no problem playing that way, but you need to answer the consequences...Maybe somebody needs to grab him and give it to him one time."

BLACKHAWKS AGITATOR **ADAM BURISH**, ON ALEX OVECHKIN.

"I am predicting somebody's going to get him. And somebody's going to get him good. There's somebody out there—some big defenseman is going to be sitting in the weeds. As he cuts across center ice, somebody's going to cut him in half."

DON CHERRY ON ALEX OVECHKIN

"Like it or lump it, that's what he does. Some people like it, some people don't. Personally, I don't like it."

PENGUIN **SIDNEY CROSBY**, ON ALEX OVECHKIN'S FLAMBOYANT STYLE

"He's Pavel Bure in Mark Messier's body."

CAPITALS GM **GEORGE MCPHEE**, ON OVECHKIN

"Every night the guy does something that will wow you. He may not have a great game every time, but if he's not scoring, he's hitting, and if he's not hitting, he's scoring."

CAPITALS COACH **BRUCE BOUDREAU**, ON OVECHKIN'S PROWESS

"I'm okay. Russian machine never breaks."

ALEX OVECHKIN, AFTER BEING STRUCK WITH A PUCK

"Well, he probably has sensitive skin, no?"

ALEX OVECHKIN, TRYING TO CONVINCE A REFEREE NOT TO GIVE HIS TEAMMATE A MAJOR PENALTY FOR A HIGH STICK THAT DREW BLOOD

"I wear tinted visor not to trick other players, but so hot girls in stands don't see me looking at them."

ALEX OVECHKIN, ON HIS CHOICE OF EYE PROTECTION

"Right now I'm scoring goals and I'm the king of the world. And a couple weeks ago I was almost in the toilet. **So maybe you just forget to flush me.**"

CAPITAL ALEX OVECHKIN

"You'll never catch me bragging about goals, but I'll talk all you want about my assists."

OILER **WAYNE GRETZKY**

"I sometimes think that if you part Wayne's hair you'll find another eye."

GORDIE HOWE ON **WAYNE GRETZKY**

"Gretzky is like an invisible man. He appears out of nowhere, passes to nowhere, and a goal is scored."

IGOR DMITRIEV, A COACH OF THE SOVIET NATIONAL HOCKEY TEAM

"There should be a league rule where he is passed around from team to team each year."

BRUINS COACH **TERRY O'REILLY**, AFTER GRETZKY HELPED EDMONTON SWEEP THE BRUINS IN THE 1988 STANLEY CUP FINALS

"The only way you can check Gretzky is to hit him when he is standing still singing the national anthem."

BRUINS GM **HARRY SINDEN**

"**The hardest thing for me has always been that I've been compared to myself.**"

RANGER WAYNE GRETZKY

"**What kind of hair did Mel Gibson have in Braveheart? It's warrior hair and hockey players are warriors.**"

BROADCASTER **BARRY MELROSE**,
WHO WEARS A MULLET, ON THE CONTINUING
POPULARITY OF HIS HAIRSTYLE IN HOCKEY

"My hair was too big. And my head is big, and my hair is big, so my helmet gets too small. So I have to make a haircut."

CAPITAL **ALEX OVECHKIN**

"If Jaromir Jagr can wear a mullet for eight years, why can't I wear a Mohawk?"

LEAF **BRYAN McCABE**, ON CRITICISM OVER HIS NEW HAIRSTYLE

"I remember taking a look at him and saying, 'Anyone who perms his hair has got to go.' So we sent him to Fort Worth."

DON CHERRY, ON COACHING DON SALESKI IN COLORADO

"It would hurt attendance."

DEVIL **MIKE PELUSO**, ON WHY HE WOULDN'T
CUT HIS SHOULDER-LENGTH HAIR

· 87 ·

"I wouldn't urinate in his ear if his brain was on fire."

HALL OF FAME BLACKHAWK **BOBBY HULL**,
ON A LONGTIME MONTREAL RIVAL

"I'm kind of happy he's not. I didn't want to see him. I just hate the guy... I can't lie, sorry."

PENGUIN **MAX TALBOT**, WHEN ASKED ABOUT ALEX OVECHKIN NOT BEING IN PITTSBURGH FOR THE SUMMERTIME PRESS CONFERENCE ANNOUNCING THE 2011 WINTER CLASSIC

"As much as you hate a team like Colorado, you love to play 'em. The juices will be boiling, and the blood will be flowing. Let's clarify that: flowing through your body. Not on the ice."

WING **KRIS DRAPER**, ON AN UPCOMING PLAYOFF SERIES AGAINST THE AVALANCHE

"Anybody I can't stand to play against, I would like to play with."

FLYER **ERIC LINDROS**, ON PLAYING WITH CLAUDE LEMIEUX AND BRENDAN SHANAHAN FOR TEAM CANADA

"Rocket had that mean look on, every game we played. He was 100 percent hockey. He could hate with the best of them."

HALL OF FAME RED WING **GORDIE HOWE**, ON MAURICE RICHARD

"At least I don't need a mask for Halloween now."

SENATOR **ANDREAS DACKELL**, AFTER SUFFERING A
CONCUSSION AND FACIAL CUTS THAT REQUIRED
30 STITCHES

"They had to take a time out to do some repairs to
the boards."

BRUIN **DON SWEENEY**, ON TAKING STICHES IN HIS HEAD
AFTER HE LOST HIS BALANCE IN A SKILLS COMPETITION

"Believe me, I know the difference between a stick
and a glove."

OILER **DAVE ROBERTS**, AFTER SUSTAINING A BROKEN
NOSE AND CHEEKBONE PLUS AN ORBITAL FRACTURE
FROM RANGER MARK MESSIER'S CROSS-CHECK, ON THE
NHL RULING THAT HIS INJURIES WERE CAUSED BY
MESSIER'S GLOVE RATHER THAN HIS STICK

"I tried to use my head to hurt his hand."

SENATOR **ALEXEI KOVALEV**, ON HIS FIGHT WITH LEAFS
DEFENSEMAN FRANÇOIS BEAUCHEMIN

"Tell him he's Wayne Gretzky."

OILERS COACH **TED GREEN**, AFTER OILER SHAUN VAN ALLEN
SUFFERED A CONCUSSION AND COULDN'T REMEMBER WHO
HE WAS

"It's nice to get a standing ovation in Montreal."

PANTHER SCOTT MELLANBY, WHO WAS KNOCKED
UNCONSCIOUS AFTER SLIDING AND HITTING THE
BACK OF HIS HEAD ON THE BOARDS, ON THE APPLAUSE
HE RECEIVED AS HE WAS CARRIED OFF THE ICE ON
A STRETCHER

"His eyes are wide open and he looks alert. He might be a goalie."

DUCKS GOALIE **DOMINIC ROUSSEL**, ON PARENTING

"I think you look tougher, more grizzled, without teeth. My kids tell me the same thing. If they're not behaving around the house, I'll take the teeth out and keep 'em in line."

WILD'S **WES WALZ**, ON HIS BABY DAUGHTER

"Trade Steve Yzerman? That's like asking me if I want to trade my son Jason for the kid next door."

WINGS COACH **JACQUES DEMERS**

"My daughter Chelsea, 12, really knows players. She looked at a book and picked out the cutest guy and said we had to take this Ilya Kovalchuk. She was right."

THRASHERS GM **DON WADDELL**, ON THE THRASHERS' 2001 DRAFT PICK

"He asked me if he could marry Carrie before he asked her. I said, 'You want to what?' I thought he was just going to ask for more ice time."

LIGHTNING GM **PHIL ESPOSITO**, ON HIS DAUGHTER MARRYING LIGHTNING ALEXANDER SELIVANOV

"Daddy, you're the best hockey player in the world except that you can't score."

CLANCY WILLIAMS, SIX-YEAR-OLD DAUGHTER OF
CANUCK DAVE "TIGER" WILLIAMS, DURING A SCORING SLUMP

"We know that hockey is where we live, where we can best meet and overcome pain and wrong and death. Life is just a place where we spend time between games."

FLYERS COACH **FRED SHERO**

"I've always felt hockey was like a disease. You can't really shake it."

FLAMES GOALIE **KEN WREGGET**

"Hockey is a man's game. The team with the most real men wins."

CANUCKS GM **BRIAN BURKE**

"You have to know what pro hockey is all about. You have to live and breathe and sleep it. You have to lose a few teeth and take some shots to the face. It's not a pretty thing."

SABRES COACH **TED NOLAN**

"Hockey is like a religion in Montreal. You're either a saint or a sinner, there's no in-between."

AVALANCHE AND FORMER CANADIENS GOALIE
PATRICK ROY

"Our dreams and thoughts were always to one day lift this trophy. When you do it's a fact and no one can ever take that away from you."

OILER **WAYNE GRETZKY**

"Nothing is permanent in this business until you have the Stanley Cup perched on the trophy shelf."

HALL OF FAME COACH AND GM **TOMMY IVAN**

"This is the only thing that has seen more parties than us."

STEVEN TYLER, AEROSMITH'S LEAD SINGER, ON THE STANLEY CUP

"If we do win this thing, that Cup's going to be beside me at the altar. I hope the wife doesn't get too mad."

CAPITAL **OLAF KOLZIG**, ON HIS UPCOMING WEDDING

"Tasted like horse pee from a tin cup."

HALL OF FAME CANADIEN GOALIE GUMP WORSLEY,
ON DRINKING CHAMPAGNE FROM THE STANLEY CUP

"It's going to be nice to be embarrassed in practice instead of games."

PANTHER **RHETT WARRENER,** ON HAVING PAVEL BURE BECOME A TEAMMATE

"I scored my hat trick. One by hand, one by foot, one by mistake."

WING **SLAVA KOZLOV**, AFTER HE SCORED TWO GOALS,
HAD TWO DISALLOWED AND WAS CALLED FOR GOALIE
INTERFERENCE ON A WAVED-OFF GOAL BY TEAMMATE
STEVE YZERMAN

"Sorry is not something you get to say. Sorry is what you become."

LEAFS GM **BRIAN BURKE**

"The scum of the league really came through tonight."

LEAF **ALYN McCAULEY**, AFTER HE, TIE DOMI
AND JYRKI LUMME SCORED IN TORONTO'S 3-1 WIN
OVER CHICAGO

"Even a blind dog finds a bone once in a while."

BLUE **KELLY CHASE**, AFTER THE ENFORCER SCORED
TWICE IN 33 SECONDS AND ADDED AN ASSIST
IN A 5-1 WIN AGAINST PREDATORS

"Was Wayne Gretzky sick?"

CANADIEN **LARRY ROBINSON**, AFTER BEING NAMED
NHL PLAYER OF THE WEEK

"We get nose jobs
all the time
in the NHL,
and we don't even have
to go to the hospital."

HALL OF FAME BRUIN BRAD PARK

"The purchase of the motorcycle is on hold."

SENATOR **RON TUGNUTT**, AFTER SUFFERING
TWO CRACKED RIBS IN A BOATING ACCIDENT
AND BEING IN TWO CAR ACCIDENTS

"I knew I was in trouble when I heard snap, crackle and pop, and I wasn't having a bowl of cereal."

LEAF **NICK KYPREOS**, AFTER SUFFERING
A SPIRAL ANKLE FRACTURE IN A FIGHT

"I just tape four Tylenols to it."

OILER **BORIS MIRONOV**, ON PLAYING WITH A SORE ANKLE

"It's no big deal. Like Gordie Howe says, elbows are to hockey players what fenders are to cars."

CANADIAN **ERIC LINDROS**, ON HAVING HIS ELBOW DRAINED
DURING THE 1996 WORLD CUP

"I could hardly skate. I was taped up like a thoroughbred but I was moving like a Clydesdale."

LEAF **DEREK KING**, ON PLAYING THROUGH INJURIES

"Sounds better than hurting yourself eating pancakes."

SENATOR **DANIEL ALFREDSSON**, ON TEAMMATE CRAIG
ANDERSON INJURING HIMSELF CUTTING A FROZEN CHICKEN
BREAST WEEKS AFTER L.A. KING DUSTIN PENNER HURT HIS
BACK EATING PANCAKES

"I think I might get 1,000 stitches before I get to 1,000 points."

COYOTE **JEREMY ROENICK**, AFTER TAKING
A GASH TO THE FACE

"Most people who don't know I play hockey think I was thrown through a plate-glass window or something."

FLAME **THEO FLEURY**, ON THE 500 STITCHES
HE HAS RECEIVED IN HIS CAREER

"I was kind of hoping it would straighten it out. One of these times it will."

FLYER **ROD BRIND'AMOUR**, AFTER SUFFERING HIS FOURTH
BROKEN NOSE

"When we think he has run out of incredible things to do, he does something incredible again. You wonder how much better the kid can get."

PENGUINS COACH **KEVIN CONSTANTINE**, ON JAROMIR JAGR

"The only way we could have, was to have shot him before the game started."

FLAMES COACH **BRIAN SUTTER**, ON HOW HIS TEAM COULD HAVE STOPPED JAROMIR JAGR

"There are probably four ways to play Jagr, all of them wrong. He's the toughest player in hockey to devise a game plan against."

BLUE JACKETS COACH **DAVE KING**

"When I said, 'Hey Dad, we lost the game, but we played good,' he always said, 'You're not a figure skater, you don't get points by looking good. You have to score a goal.' When I played against other six-year-olds, I was great. When I played against 10-year-olds, I was average. He wanted me to play where I was average."

DEVIL **JAROMIR JAGR**

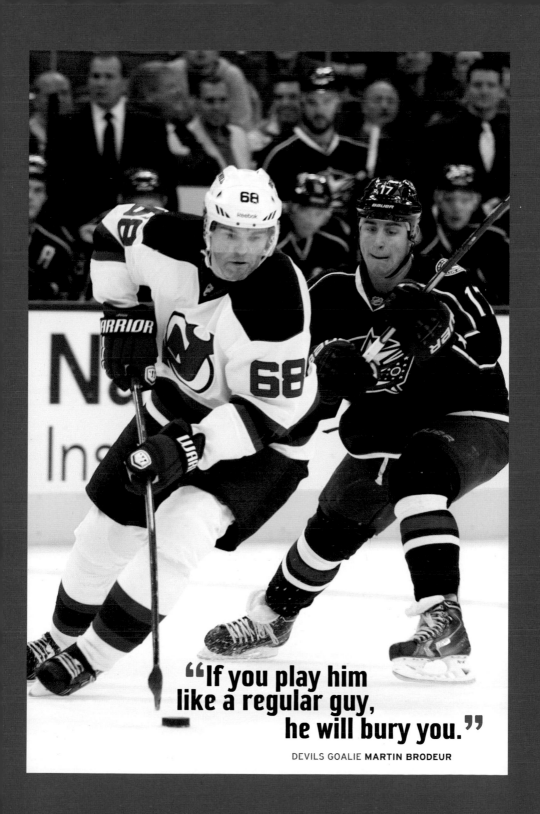

"If you play him like a regular guy, he will bury you."

DEVILS GOALIE **MARTIN BRODEUR**

"We only speak two languages here: English and profanity."

PENGUINS COACH **KEVIN CONSTANTINE**, ON THE MANY NATIVE LANGUAGES SPOKEN BY HIS TEAM

"Esa talks twice as much as anybody else. That's because you can understand just half what he says."

OILER **CRAIG MACTAVISH**, ON FINNISH TEAMMATE ESA TIKKANEN

"He's one of those guys whose English gets worse every year. But as long as it doesn't affect his play, we're all right."

LEAF **WADE BELAK**, ON CZECH TEAMMATE TOMAS KABERLE'S THICK ACCENT

"I say no words... I can't speak with him. I shy. He too good."

WING **PAVEL DATSYUK**, ON GORDIE HOWE

"Proceeds go to a translator for Alex Burrows."

CANUCK **KEVIN BIEKSA**, ON TEAMMATE RYAN KESLER'S CLOTHING LINE

"Hell, I don't know if he speaks French."

CANADIENS COACH **TOE BLAKE**, WHEN ASKED IF QUIET ROOKIE HENRI RICHARD SPOKE ANY ENGLISH

"We're scared of losing. That's why we win. We know what it's like to lose and we hate it. We enjoy being champions too much."

ISLANDER **BOB BOURNE**, ON HIS TEAM'S FOUR STANLEY CUP WINS IN THE 1980S

"It means that we're in the basement."

RANGERS COACH **MICHEL BERGERON**, ASKED BY A REPORTER WHAT THE TEAM'S 14 LOSSES BY A 1-GOAL MARGIN MEANT

"Potential is synonymous with getting your ass kicked."

PENGUINS COACH **KEVIN CONSTANTINE**, ASKED IF HIS TEAM HAD POTENTIAL

"If you're a good loser, you're a loser."

CANUCKS COACH **JOHN TORTORELLA**

"It seems like we're doing just enough to lose by a little."

KING **AARON MILLER**, ON HIS TEAM'S 3-12-0-1 FUNK

"It's the nuts and bolts time of the year and we don't have enough nuts and bolts."

SHARKS COACH **DARRYL SUTTER**, ON A LATE-SEASON LOSING STREAK

"A complacent player is a lazy player, and a lazy player is a loser."

BLACKHAWKS COACH **DARRYL SUTTER**

"I don't order fries with my club sandwich."

PENGUIN **MARIO LEMIEUX**, TO TEAMMATE RON FRANCIS,
WHO ASKED HIM WHAT HE DID TO STAY IN SHAPE IN THE
OFF-SEASON

"One thing I hate is people screaming at me. If
you want me to do something, talk to me. When
someone screams at me to hurry up, I slow down."

PENGUIN **MARIO LEMIEUX**

"Usually when you play a team, you want to focus
on one line. Pittsburgh is the only team where you
have to focus on one player. When he's coming
toward you, all you see is him."

CANADIENS GOALIE **PATRICK ROY**

"There's no book on Mario. It's not like he has a
favorite thing that he does over and over. Every
time it's a different adventure. And you know that
if he does the things that he wants to do, the puck's
going to go in the net."

WHALERS GOALIE **PETER SIDORKIEWICZ**

"His face is so calm. He shows no sign of stress or anything. It's as if he's saying, 'No problem. Relax. I'm just going to beat you now. It's not going to hurt a bit.'" FLYERS GOALIE DOMINIC ROUSSEL

"The only pressure I'm under is the pressure I've put on myself."

RANGER **MARK MESSIER**

"I started as a fourth-line fighter, went to being a third-line centre, then a second-line winger and a first-line centre. I've played every role there is, and the only thing that matters is helping the team win."

RANGER **MARK MESSIER**

"When he gets mad, it's like he's in another world. He'll look at you with those big eyes and they'll be going around in circles."

RETIRED RANGER **BARRY BECK**,
ON MARK MESSIER

"He ran over a few people, nothing major. Mess runs over people. Sometimes, people don't get up. That's life."

HALL OF FAME GOALIE **GRANT FUHR**, ON
MARK MESSIER

Biologically, I'm 10.
Chronologically, I'm 33.
In hockey years, I'm 66."

RANGER MARK MESSIER, IN 1994

"If you're built like a freight train, you can't drive around like a Volkswagen."

HALL OF FAME ISLANDER **CLARK GILLIES**,
ON UNDERACHIEVING ISLANDER
TODD BERTUZZI

"It's much easier to slow down a thoroughbred than have to kick a donkey to get him going."

THRASHERS COACH **BOB HARTLEY**, ON NOT WANTING
TO REIN IN SNIPER ILYA KOVALCHUK TOO MUCH

"I'd rather tame a tiger than paint stripes on a kitty cat."

SHARKS GM **DEAN LOMBARDI**, ON OBTAINING
FREQUENTLY SUSPENDED BRYAN MARCHMENT

"It's like he's parting the Red Sea. He gives them an opening, but most of the scorers wind up drowning.

WHALERS COACH **PAUL HOLMGREN**, ON SEAN BURKE

"A hockey player without a stick is like a duck without wings."

RETIRED RED WING AND DETROIT BROADCASTER
MICKEY REDMOND

"I looked like a big stiff [on television]. What a sobering experience. I always thought of myself as Nureyev on ice. But on TV, I realized that I was a dump truck.

I was an
elep

hant
on wheels."

HALL OF FAME CANADIENS GOALIE **KEN DRYDEN**

"Hmm, 600 games? What does it mean? It means I'm that much closer to getting fired."

WILD COACH **JACQUES LEMAIRE**, AFTER
COACHING HIS 600TH GAME

"I just think it's great for David. I think it's terrific. Things like that don't bother me. When I retired, I was third in the league in scoring all-time. If I can live long enough, I might be 100th."

LIGHTNING ANNOUNCER **PHIL ESPOSITO**, ON LIGHTNING
DAVE ANDREYCHUK TYING HIS NHL RECORD OF 249 POWER
PLAY GOALS

"People don't remember records. They remember milestones."

LIGHTNING **DAVE ANDREYCHUK**, ONE GOAL AWAY FROM
TYING PHIL ESPOSITO'S RECORD 249 POWER-PLAY GOALS,
ON WHY HE'D RATHER SCORE HIS 600TH CAREER GOAL

"All that means is that I'll be 783 years old when I catch Scotty Bowman."

PENGUINS COACH **KEVIN CONSTANTINE**, AFTER BEING
CONGRATULATED ON HIS 100TH CAREER WIN

"You want to stick around the league and make a name for yourself. Steve Larmer once told me getting here is the easier part. Staying here is the hard part. He's been right for 15 years."

FLYER **JEREMY ROENICK**, AFTER PLAYING HIS
1,000TH CAREER GAME, ON ADVICE FROM
HIS FORMER BLACKHAWK TEAMMATE

"I'd have to answer to my mom."

PANTHER **ROB NIEDERMAYER,** ON WHAT WOULD
HAPPEN IF HE BOARDED HIS BROTHER SCOTT

"My mom, she keeps telling me she wants a goal.
I tell her: 'Hey Mom, I'm tryin', I'm tryin', every
day.'"

BRUIN **PJ STOCK**

"I told her they must all be sold out."

LEAF **WADE BELAK**, ON HIS RESPONSE WHEN HIS MOTHER
SAID SHE COULDN'T FIND HIS SWEATER FOR SALE AT THE
AIR CANADA CENTRE'S SOUVENIR SHOP

"Optimistically, you hope someday you'll be in a
magazine. Of course, your mom hopes it's *Sports
Illustrated* or something like that."

AVALANCHE **DAN HINOTE**, ON BEING INTERVIEWED IN
PENTHOUSE MAGAZINE

"He was mild-mannered and I don't know how he
ever got into the tough-role business. He was not a
rough kid. The rough stuff must have come from
his mother's side of the family."

WAYNE LANGDON, ON SON CANUCK ENFORCER
DARREN LANGDON

"I won't miss him. Maybe the West Edmonton Mall will miss him, but not me."

OILERS GM **GLEN SATHER**, ON LEAVING HIGHLY PAID UNDERACHIEVER ANDREI KOVALENKO EXPOSED IN THE EXPANSION DRAFT

"Lunch is on me."

WING **BRENDAN SHANAHAN**, AFTER SIGNING A $26-MILLION CONTRACT

"Bert's wallet is like an onion. Any time he opens it, he starts crying."

CANUCK **BRENDAN MORRISON**, ON TEAMMATE TODD BERTUZZI

"Players' salaries have been on the space shuttle and coaches' salaries have been on the escalator."

FLYERS COACH **TERRY MURRAY**

"I would cry a lot, so I try not to think about it."

HALL OF FAME PLAYER **BRAD PARK**, ASKED WHAT HE
WOULD EARN IN TODAY'S GAME

"Today I might be making eight or 10 million bucks.
But that's okay. You can only eat one steak at a
time, drink one beer and play one round of golf at
a time. So it doesn't mean you can't live your life
and enjoy it. Money's not what makes you happy."

HALL OF FAME LEAF **DARRYL SITTLER**

"To get my paycheque for two weeks, my family must work 200 years in Slovakia."

BLUE **PAVOL DEMITRA**, ON HIS
$1.1-MILLION SALARY

"Forget about style; worry about results."

HALL OF FAME BRUIN **BOBBY ORR**

"I believe Bobby Orr had the greatest impact of any
player to come along in my lifetime. He earned his
place in hockey history by single handedly changing
the game from the style played in my day. In my
mind there can be no greater legacy."

HALL OF FAME CANADIEN **JEAN BELIVEAU**

"I don't think you ever stopped Bobby Orr. You
contained Bobby Orr, but you never stopped him.
When we played the Bruins and Bobby had to give
up the puck, it was a good play."

HALL OF FAME CANADIEN **LARRY ROBINSON**

"The first thing I would do when I saw Bobby
coming down at me was to say a little prayer if
I had time. I'm sure I wasn't the only goalie who
did that."

HALL OF FAME LEAF **JOHNNY BOWER**

"If I can be half the hockey player that Bobby Orr
was, I'll be happy."

BRUIN **RAY BOURQUE**

"I always tell Bobby he was up in the air for so long that I had time to shower and change before he hit the ice."

HALL OF FAME BLUES GOALIE GLENN HALL, ON BOBBY ORR'S FAMOUS GOAL TO WIN THE 1970 STANLEY CUP

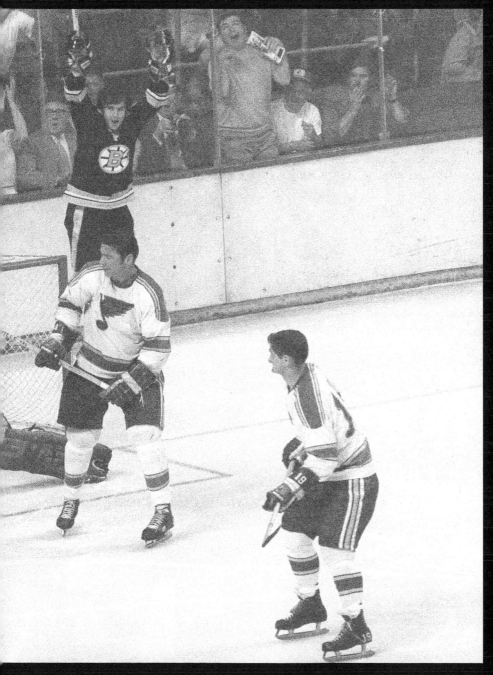

"When you hit him, it was like running into a bag of anvils."

DON CHERRY, ON LEAF EDDIE SHACK, WHOM HE PLAYED AGAINST IN THE AHL

"Players today put too much emphasis on lifting weights, low body fat and big muscles that they think make them look good—all that bullshit. What you need to play hockey is heart and determination, and the ability to stay mentally strong. Mental strength beats physical strength any day."

HALL OF FAME CENTER **PHIL ESPOSITO**

"This dressing room is like a wing of the Hall of Fame: Hasek, Shanahan, Yzerman, Hull, Robitaille, Larionov, Chelios, Lidstrom. All these All-Stars and future Hall of Famers, and then you come to me—reality."

WING **KRIS DRAPER**

"I remember my first NHL game against him. 'Don't mess with me, old man,' I told him. Next thing I remember was the smelling salts."

"I didn't know whether to stay for two or five."

RETIRED BRUIN **TERRY O'REILLY**, WHO JOKINGLY WENT
TO THE PENALTY BOX RATHER THAN CENTER ICE AT
THE CEREMONY RETIRING HIS NUMBER.

"It's the first time that I can recall calling a bench
minor penalty that really fit the crime."

DEVIL **MARTIN BRODEUR**, AFTER NEW JERSEY COACH
ROBBIE FTOREK THREW A BENCH IN ANGER ABOUT A
PENALTY CALL

"Hey Paul, we should've gone. We'd have only got
five [minutes]."

SABRE **ROB RAY**, TO PANTHER PAUL LAUS FROM
THE PENALTY BOX, AFTER HE AND LAUS WERE GIVEN
TEN-MINUTE MISCONDUCTS FOR NOT ENDING A SCRUM

"I'm glad it's him and not some other puke."

RETIRED **DAVE "TIGER" WILLIAMS**, AFTER MAPLE
LEAF TIE DOMI BROKE WILLIAMS'S TORONTO CAREER
PENALTY MINUTES RECORD

"Where are you putting the penalty box?"

LEAF **TIE DOMI,** ASKING HIS FIRST QUESTION DURING HIS TOUR OF THE AIR CANADA CENTRE UNDER CONSTRUCTION

"I never knew the rules.
I used common sense.
It's really the only way
to run a game.
If officials called
every penalty they saw,
there would be
no players on the ice
and no one in the rink."

HALL OF FAME REFEREE **BILL CHADWICK**

"The next time I want to criticize a referee, I'll give 10 of my players $1,000 each and get them to do it."

WINGS COACH **SCOTTY BOWMAN**, AFTER RECEIVING A $10,000 FINE

"I don't make enough money at this point to get into the specifics."

HURRICANES GOALIE **KEVIN WEEKES**, ON DECLINING TO GIVE DETAILS ON OFFICIATING

"It's too bad it wasn't a brick."

SABRES COACH **JIM SCHOENFELD**, AFTER TOSSING A WATER BOTTLE AT REFEREE TERRY GREGSON

"It's the first time a ref ever listened to me."

DUCKS GOALIE **GUY HEBERT**, AFTER REFEREE DAN MAROUELLI TOOK HIS REQUEST, WENT FOR VIDEO REVIEW AND DENIED A GOAL

"**First they give him two, then it's five, then a game [misconduct]. I was wondering whether the electric chair was next.**"

HURRICANES COACH **PAUL MAURICE**, ON ERIK COLE'S
HIT ON OTTAWA'S CHRIS PHILLIPS

"Have you ever seen one of these things back into a mountain?"

BLACKHAWK **DOUG JARRETT**, ON WHY HE ALWAYS
REQUESTED THE LAST ROW ON AN AIRPLANE

"My wife always laughs that I pack about 20 pairs of underwear and I come back home and 19 of them are untouched."

CANUCK **DARCY HORDICHUK**, ON HIS TENDENCY TO OVER
PACK AND UNDER USE HIS CLOTHES

"Antti doesn't even know if he's in Canada or the U.S. right now."

BLACKHAWK **BRIAN CAMPBELL**, ON THE NARROW
FOCUS OF HIS TEAM'S FINNISH GOALTENDER,
ANTTI NIEMII

"We bring the fathers in and they get to spend some time on the road. They can see the babysitting I have to do."

LEAFS COACH **RANDY CARLYLE**, ON THE LEAFS'
FATHER-SON ROAD TRIP

"Hey, I'm from Fort Saskatchewan, Alberta. It makes Buffalo look like Rome."

LEAF **JOFFREY LUPUL**, IN APOLOGY AFTER HE MADE FUN OF THE VIEW FROM HIS BUFFALO HOTEL ROOM ON TWITTER

"I usually call the new guy and let him know where I like to sit on the bus, tell him ways he can stay out of my way, make sure he knows not to touch any of my stuff"

WING **BRENDAN SHANAHAN**, ON GETTING A NEW TEAMMATE

"It's definitely weird coming back for one game and then going right out again. It really is like Edmonton is just another stop on the road trip, except Ryan Nugent-Hopkins and I share a house together and we spent our time here doing all our laundry. It was a very grown up sort of day for us."

SECOND-YEAR OILER STAR **JUSTIN SCHULTZ**, ON ROAD TRIPS IN THE WESTERN CONFERENCE

"**Enjoy the reception.**
Don't break
anything."

PRESIDENT **BARACK OBAMA**, TO THE STANLEY CUP CHAMPION
CHICAGO BLACKHAWKS, DURING THEIR VISIT TO THE WHITE HOUSE

"I was so excited. I was 26 and I didn't think I was ever going to make it to the NHL. I forgot that I was there to stop pucks."

RANGER **ED GIACOMIN**, ON HIS DISAPPOINTING 1965–66
ROOKIE SEASON

"This is a first."

LEAFS COACH **MIKE MURPHY**, AFTER ROOKIE JEFF WARE
NEEDED A NOTE FOR THE TEACHER IN ORDER TO BE
EXCUSED FROM HIS UNIVERSITY OF TORONTO PSYCHOLOGY
CLASS EXAM

"We're going to find out who did it, and probably do nothing about it."

PENGUIN **BEN LOVEJOY**, AFTER THE HOTEL FURNITURE
FROM THE ROOM BELONGING TO HIM AND FELLOW ROOKIE
MARK LETESTU WAS SET UP IN THE HALLWAY AS A PRANK
BY HIS TEAMMATES

"I'm a teenager so, technically, my dad can still ground me."

LEAF **MORAGN RIELLY**, ON THE PARTYING THAT MAY
OR MAY NOT HAPPEN DURING TORONTO'S FATHER-SON
ROAD TRIP

"I'm trying to act like every other guy, but inside there is a party going on."

AVALANCHE **JEFF DAW**, ON BEING CALLED UP
BY COLORADO FOR HIS FIRST NHL GAME AFTER
FIVE-AND-A-HALF YEARS IN THE MINORS

"I look out there during the warm-ups and I see Brett Hull and Niklas Lidstrom and Brendan Shanahan and Sergei Fedorov. I'm used to playing these guys in video games and here I am about to play against them for real. It was a dream come true."

WILD'S **STEPHANE VEILLEUX**, ON MAKING HIS NHL DEBUT
AGAINST DETROIT

"We're at the home of one of the richest guys on the planet and he's got one of the best wine collections in the world and nobody's drinking it but me. I look around and the kids are all playing Tiger Woods' PlayStation."

PANTHER **STEPHANE MATTEAU**, AFTER A VISIT TO THE
OWNER'S MANSION, ON HOW YOUNG HIS TEAMMATES ARE

"I'm not crazy, I'm Russian."

LEAF DIMITRI YUSHKEVICH

"The Cold War is back on."

SENATOR **SHAWN McEACHERN**, ON TEAMMATE ALEXEI
YASHIN'S AGENT CLAIMING BIGOTRY

"This is definitely the best team I have played [on]
in the National Hockey League, but in Russia, the
teams I played for were some of the best teams
in the history of the game."

WING **IGOR LARIONOV**, WHO PLAYED FOR RUSSIAN OLYMPIC
AND WORLD CHAMPIONSHIP GOLD MEDAL TEAMS

"I had a few fights last year, but I need to take
boxing lessons. I need to, because in the NHL it's
required."

KING **MAXIM KUZNETSOV**, ON ENTERING THE NHL

"There is no position in sport as noble as goaltending."

HALL OF FAME SOVIET UNION NATIONAL TEAM GOALIE
VLADISLAV TRETIAK

"I can't say even if I did know, because it's a big secret. I'm still in the KGB."

WING **PAVEL DATSYUK**, ON WHY RUSSIAN COACH SLAVA BYKOV
HAD BEEN SO SUCCESSFUL PRIOR TO VANCOUVER 2010

"As a child there were three horror films we knew from the West. One was *Nightmare on Elm Street*, the second one was *Friday the 13th* – and the third one was *Miracle on Ice*."

RUSSIAN SOCHI ORGANIZING COMMITTEE HEAD
DMITRY CHERNYSHENKO

"After I thank God at night for having a great wife, I say a quiet prayer for having those two guys on my team."

CAPITALS COACH **GLEN HANLON**, EXPRESSING HIS GRATITUDE FOR
YOUNG RUSSIAN STARS ALEX OVECHKIN AND ALEX SEMIN

"We didn't have any trouble communicating on the ice, no matter how fast we played. Hockey was just fun. On that line, I played defensively and would back-check. As soon as we got the puck, I would find either Alex or Pavel with a good pass and the puck would be in the net before I crossed the blue line."

BLUE JACKET **SERGEI FEDOROV**, ON HIS PRE-NHL EXPERIENCE
PLAYING FOR THE RUSSIAN NATIONAL TEAM ON A LINE WITH
ALEXANDER MOGILNY AND PAVEL BURE

"I've never had major knee surgery on any other part of my body."

CANADIEN **SAKU KOIVU**, TO REPORTERS

"I was young and stupid then. Now I'm not young anymore."

LEAF **JYRKI LUMME**, ON HIS EARLY YEARS
WITH MONTREAL

"Playing with Steve Guolla is like playing with myself."

SHARK **JEFF FRIESEN**, ON HIS TEAMMATE

"Those were little monumental mistakes."

CANADIENS COACH **JEAN PERRON**

"That's a whole new ball of worms."

HURRICANE ROD BRIND'AMOUR, UPSET AFTER DOCTORS
FOUND A SECOND BREAK IN HIS LEFT FOOT

"Getting cut in the face is a pain in the butt."

FLAME THEO FLEURY

"We have only one person to blame, and that's each other."

RANGER BARRY BECK, AFTER A LOSS

"He's the kind of guy who will stab you in the back right to your face."

BLUE BRETT HULL, ON COACH MIKE KEENAN

"You hit the head right on the nail."

SABRE BRIAN HOLZINGER, DURING A
FIRST INTERMISSION INTERVIEW

"Wave it high and don't trip."

SIDNEY CROSBY GIVING ADVICE TO WOMEN'S HOCKEY STAR HAYLEY WICKENHEISER, ON BEING CANADA'S FLAG BEARER AT THE SOCHI OLYMPICS

"The guys always give me a hard time about Bon Jovi."

SIDNEY CROSBY, ON HIS CD COLLECTION

"What I can say about him? He is a good player, but he talks too much."

CAPITAL **ALEX OVECHKIN**, ON SIDNEY CROSBY'S COMPLAINING

"I'll be the first one to admit, my first couple of years I was pretty hard on the refs."

SIDNEY CROSBY, ON HIS COMPLAINING TO THE REFS

"He was no secret: At 15, we knew he was the next great one ... He keeps you on the edge of your seat. He gets off the ice, you can't wait to see him get back on."

PENGUINS SCOUT AND GOALIE COACH **GILLES MELOCHE**, ON SIDNEY CROSBY

" I've won the Stanley Cup, won gold medals. Getting Sidney Crosby was the happiest day of my life. "

PENGUINS EXEC **CRAIG PATRICK**, ON DRAFTING SIDNEY CROSBY

"You're not going to intimidate this kid. He's not going to back off. There are players like that. When we played against Henri Richard or Frank Mahovlich, the word at our meetings was leave those guys alone. Ask them how their families are doing, but don't wake them up. If you tick them off, they become even better players."

PENGUINS EXEC AND FORMER NHL GOALIE **ED JOHNSTON**, ON SIDNEY CROSBY

"He was yelling pretty urgently. There's different pitches of yell and he was screaming."

TEAM CANADA'S **JAROME IGINLA,** ON SIDNEY CROSBY
CALLING FOR THE PUCK PRIOR TO SCORING THE OVERTIME
GAME-WINNER IN THE GOLD MEDAL GAME AT THE 2010 OLYMPICS

"**That 100-foot skate to the bench after you have been pulled is the longest, slowest skate in the world. It seems like five miles.**"

RETIRED SHARK KELLY HRUDEY,
ON A GOALIE GETTING THE HOOK MIDGAME

"Some guys score and some guys don't. We got a lot
that don't."

WINGS COACH **MIKE BABCOCK**

"I have a bull's-eye on my whole body."

PENGUIN **DARIUS KASPARAITIS**, ASKED IF HE WAS
PREPARED FOR OPPONENTS TO ACT AS IF HE HAD
A BULL'S-EYE ON HIS RECENTLY HEALED KNEE

"All my career I've gone to teams on the decline.
I went to Quebec when they were losing the
Stastny brothers. I went to Edmonton after they lost
Gretzky and Messier. I went to Anaheim when it
was an expansion team. I came to Montreal after
they'd won the Cup and were headed down. I was
beginning to think it was me."

SENATOR **RON TUGNUTT**

"I just don't know what to think. I play in Colorado,
they tell me they like me, and I get traded. I play in
Calgary, and at the end of the season the GM tells
me he likes me, and I get traded. I just hope my
fiancee doesn't tell me she likes me."

SABRE **CHRIS DRURY**, AFTER TRADE FROM
CALGARY TO BUFFALO

"Wayne came over to the bench one day after seeing Chara, and said, 'That's why I'm quitting.'"

RANGERS COACH JOHN MUCKLER, LAUGHING ABOUT WAYNE GRETZKY'S COMMENT ON OTTAWA'S SIX-FOOT-NINE DEFENSEMAN ZDENO CHARA

"The goal is too small and the goalies are too big."

WINGS COACH **SCOTTY BOWMAN**, ON WHY GOALS ARE HARD
TO COME BY

"He's a mountain that moves."

COYOTE **SHANE DOAN**, ON TEAMMATE GEORGES LARAQUE

"I wish that we could tumble them in the dryer for
30 minutes and get them to shrink, but that won't
happen."

FLAMES COACH **BOB HARTLEY**, AT THE PROSPECT OF
PLAYING ANAHEIM, SAN JOSE AND LOS ANGELES ON A
ROAD TRIP

"He's not big in size, but he's big in heart."

LIGHTNING **ROB ZAMUNER**, ON TEAMMATE DARCY TUCKER

"It's hard to move 275 pounds of loose meat."

CANUCK **KEVIN BIEKSA**, ON BLACKHAWK
DUSTIN BYFUGLIEN

"The bigger they are, the harder they hit."

BRUINS ASSISTANT-GM MIKE O'CONNELL, ON ACQUIRING SIX-FOOT-FOUR, 225-POUND KEN BELANGER IN 1998

"One night he skated past me
     after winging one right by my ear.
He stopped for a second and muttered,
    'Watch out for me, Emile.
     I'm shooting a little high tonight.'
Next time he came by,
I had caught the puck and
I threw it way out to my left.
While everyone was looking over there,
    I gave him a fine two-hander
    with the lumber.
     Right across the ankles.
While they were examining him,
    laid out on the ice, I skated over.
    'Hey, I'm sorry,
     but I'm hitting a little low tonight.'"

RETIRED NHL GOALIE **EMILE FRANCIS**, ON
HOW HE HANDLED A DISRESPECTFUL SHOOTER

"If I hadn't learned to lay on a two-hander once in a while, I'd never have left Flin Flon."

FLYER **BOBBY CLARKE**, IN 1972

"Broad Street Bullies and all of a sudden he's turning Pope on us."

FLYER **JEREMY ROENICK**, ON BOBBY CLARKE'S SUGGESTION THAT TODAY'S PLAYERS USE THEIR STICKS TOO MUCH

"It's going to be good to be on his side. I'll save a lot of energy. I don't have to concentrate on whacking him. I'm pretty excited about that."

BLACKHAWK **DOUG GILMOUR**, ON JOINING EX-RIVAL CHRIS CHELIOS IN CHICAGO

"First time I've ever been this close to one without it being broken over my head."

WING **DARREN McCARTY**, AFTER BLACKHAWK CHRIS CHELIOS GOT TRADED TO DETROIT, AS HE STROLLED OVER TO THE STICK RACK AND GRABBED ONE OF CHELIOS'S STICKS

"There are two things I don't want to know: how they make hot dogs and what goes on in the NHL office."

FLYERS COACH **ROGER NEILSON**, AFTER THE NHL WARNED HIS TEAM ABOUT GOALIE RUNNING

"They kept me in the dark and every once in a while opened the door and threw manure on me."

HALL OF FAME RED WING **GORDIE HOWE**, ON HOW THE CLUB TREATED HIM LIKE A MUSHROOM AFTER MAKING HIM A TEAM EXECUTIVE

"We realized if you want to play in the sandbox, you've got to bring your toys."

STARS PRESIDENT **JIM LITES**, AFTER SIGNING MIKE MODANO TO A $43.5-MILLION DEAL

"What I've learned so far from researching is that to win the Stanley Cup, you have to make the playoffs."

CAPITALS OWNER **TED LEONSIS**

"Sometimes you do the hard work and set the table and somebody else eats the meal."

BRIAN BURKE, IN THE SEASON HE WAS FIRED AS
TORONTO GENERAL MANAGER, ON THE LEAFS FINALLY
MAKING THE PLAYOFFS

"Some GMs shop at Nieman Marcus in the summer but I shop at Wal-Mart after the season starts."

THRASHERS GM **DON WADDELL**, AFTER SIGNING
FREE AGENT GOALIE BYRON DAFOE IN JANUARY
AT A BARGAIN PRICE

"One time I was told to go down the hall, past the picture of Cinderella, and turn left. Another time I was told to go upstairs and turn right when I saw Peter Pan."

DUCKS GM **PIERRE GAUTIER**, ON WORKING AT DISNEY
HEADQUARTERS

"**You miss 100 percent of the shots you never take.**"

OILER **WAYNE GRETZKY**

"I don't fear stopping a 100 mph slap shot. I fear not stopping it!"

CANUCKS GOALIE **ROBERTO LUONGO**

"Yes, and I also like jumping out of tall buildings."

PANTHER **JOHN VANBIESBROUCK**, ASKED IF HE
ENJOYED FACING 51 SHOTS IN A GAME

"I've got to get him a Goodyear endorsement."

BLUES COACH **BOB BERRY**, ON THE AMOUNT OF RUBBER
HIS GOALIE CURTIS JOSEPH WAS FACING

"Branko, you're not going to make a lot of money unless you shoot."

COYOTES COACH **BOBBY FRANCIS**, TO COYOTE ROOKIE
BRANKO RADIVOJEVIC

"There was a Toronto Maple Leafs fan sitting next to her. But I missed by a couple of inches."

SENATOR **RYAN SHANNON**, WHO TOOK A SHOT THAT
RICOCHETED OFF THE CROSSBAR INTO THE CROWD
AND HIT HIS WIFE IN THE THIGH.

"When I look at the net,
        I don't see a goalie.

PANTHER PAVEL BURE

When I look at the net, I see two or three goalies.

PANTHER RADEK DVORAK

"My teeth weren't that good to begin with, so
hopefully I can get some better ones."

BLACKHAWK **DUNCAN KEITH**, AFTER LOSING SEVERAL
TEETH FROM A PUCK IN THE MOUTH

"Well, I've got my teeth right here in my hand."

CANUCK **MIKE SILLINGER**, TRYING TO PROVE TO REFEREE
BILL MCCREARY THAT HE WAS CROSS-CHECKED BY MAPLE
LEAF JAMIE MACOUN

"I was trying to hit him in the chest. Too bad I
missed."

BLUE JACKET **SERGE AUBIN**, ON KNOCKING OUT TWO OF
PENGUIN DARIUS KASPARAITIS'S TEETH

"I was 14 when I lost them [his front teeth]. The main
thing was, we won that game, so I was the happiest.
You hate to lose your teeth and the game, too."

HALL OF FAME FLYER **BILL BARBER**

"Daneyko got mad when Kaminski said he was going to knock his teeth out. Dano has only two teeth left, so you can't say that to Dano."

DEVILS COACH **JACQUES LEMAIRE,** ON A FIGHT BETWEEN
DEVIL KEN DANEYKO AND CAPITAL KEVIN KAMINSKI

"**Every time I get injured, my wife ends up pregnant.**"

BLACKHAWK **DOUG WILSON,**
ON TIME SPENT AT HOME

"He has a great body for a hockey player, too. I don't want this to come out wrong, but he has a great rear end."

WHALERS COACH **PAUL HOLMGREN**, ON ANDREI NIKOLISHIN

"I have to go through a couple pairs of shorts each game, but other than that, it's great."

COYOTES COACH **BOB FRANCIS**, ON THE TIGHT 2001-02 PLAYOFF RACE

"A linesman thanked me after, because he said he had to pee."

WING **JONATHAN ERICSSON**, AFTER AVOIDING OVERTIME BY SCORING A GAME-WINNING GOAL WITH FIVE SECONDS LEFT

"I'd like to thank my parents for messing around 29 years ago."

WING **MANNY LEGACE**, AFTER WINNING THE STANLEY CUP

"Looks frightening from the bench. He's going to scare his kids with that thing."

STARS COACH **KEN HITCHCOCK**, ON DALLAS STAR ROMAN TUREK'S NEW MASK

"I just wanted to see if it was legal, because when he was with us he couldn't catch a thing."

WINGS COACH **SCOTTY BOWMAN**, CLAIMING HE CALLED THE EQUIPMENT COMPANY TO FIND THE SPECS OF OILERS GOALTENDER BOB ESSENSA'S GLOVE

"Maybe they should go back to wooden sticks."

JETS GOALIE **ONDREJ PAVELEC**, SUGGESTS HANDICAPPING THE SHOOTERS AFTER THE NHL PROPOSED TO SHRINK GOALTENDING EQUIPMENT

"I don't like my hockey sticks touching other sticks, and I don't like them crossing one another, and I kind of have them hidden in the corner. I put baby powder on the ends. I think it's essentially a matter of taking care of what takes care of you."

OILER **WAYNE GRETZKY**

"Could you imagine how good Glenn Hall would have been with bigger equipment?"

CANUCKS COACH **MARC CRAWFORD**

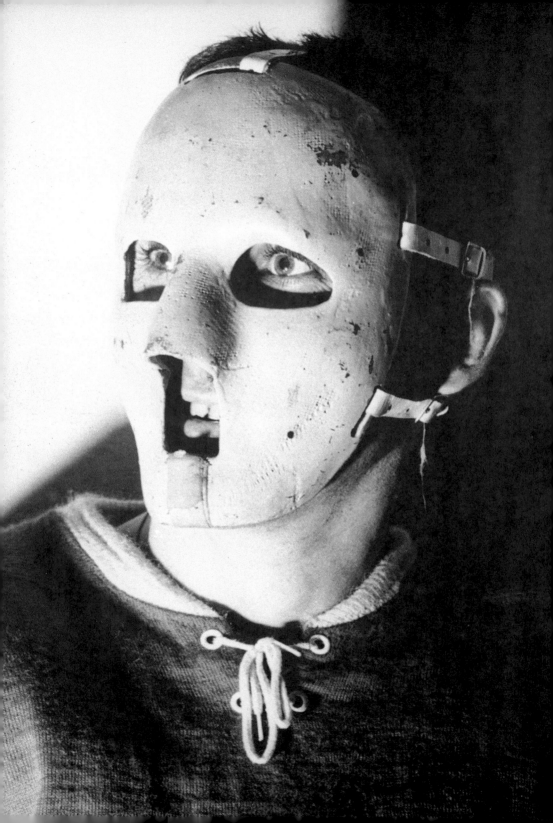

"If you jumped out of a plane without a parachute, would that prove that you were brave?"

HALL OF FAME GOALIE **JACQUES PLANTE,** ASKED IF
WEARING A MASK PROVED THAT HE WAS AFRAID

"The top three worst things I've seen in hockey? The invention of the trap. The invention of the morning skate. And the invention of the extremely

ugly

uniform."

WING BRETT HULL

"We've got no-trade clauses. Nobody wants us."

FLYER **KEITH JONES**, DESCRIBING HIMSELF AND
CRAIG BERUBE

"Really, there are none. We traded him for a 10th
round pick in a nine-round draft."

FLYERS GM **BOBBY CLARKE**, ON WHAT "FUTURE
CONSIDERATIONS" HE RECEIVED FROM THE NASHVILLE
PREDATORS FOR SERGEI KLIMENTIEV

"It's tough for a player to talk about trades, because
when a player talks about a trade that's like
throwing a teammate under the bus."

FLYER **JEREMY ROENICK**, ON HIS MIXED FEELINGS WHEN
A GOOD PLAYER IS RUMORED TO BE COMING TO HIS CLUB

"If you're winning, you'll be rewarded and if you're
losing, changes will be made. It happened when
I played and it'll happen 100 years from now."

COYOTES MANAGING PARTNER **WAYNE GRETZKY**, ON TRADES

"**I don't care if we lose every game for the next five years and the team goes broke and moves to Moose Jaw. I will not trade Pavel Bure!**"

CANUCKES GM BRIAN BURKE, SEVERAL WEEKS
BEFORE TRADING BURE TO THE PANTHERS

"The kid looks good in his first game."

WHALER **GORDIE HOWE**, AT AGE 51, AFTER 41-YEAR-OLD
BOBBY HULL MADE HIS 1979 HARTFORD WHALER DEBUT

"It was pretty weird to play against Vernie. I went to his goalie school when I was 13."

WINGS GOALIE **NORM MARACLE**, ON HIS TEAM'S 4–1 WIN
OVER SAN JOSE AND GOALIE MIKE VERNON

"That's great. I'm 100 years old and people are still interested."

BLUE **GRANT FUHR**, ON HEARING HIS NAME
IN TRADE RUMORS

"The average guy gets sophisticated when they get older and they get cynical and they think there's better things to do with their life. But not [Gordie] Howe or [Rocket] Richard. They understood that hockey was the greatest thing they'd ever do."

FLAMES ASSISTANT GM AND FORMER PLAYER **AL MacNEIL**

"He's skating like he's 36 again."

STAR **MIKE KEANE**, AFTER 38-YEAR-OLD TEAMMATE GUY
CARBONNEAU HAD A GREAT GAME

"I'll never be accused of losing a step. I'm not sure
I ever had one."

WING **LARRY MURPHY**, AT AGE 38

"He's as old as some trees."

LEAFS COACH **PAT BURNS**, ON VETERAN MAPLE LEAF MIKE
GARTNER

"I played my age. Not bad."

HURRICANE **RON FRANCIS**, AFTER PLAYING 39 MINUTES
IN THE THIRD GAME OF THE 2002 STANLEY CUP FINAL

"When no one else signs me."

WING **CHRIS CHELIOS**, ON WHEN IT WILL BE TIME
TO RETIRE

"**If they can play eight more years, then I can too. I'm in better shape than they are.**"

DUCK **TEEMU SELANNE**, 42, ON THE CONTRACT
EXTENSIONS OF RYAN GETZLAF AND COREY PERRY,
BOTH 27

"I thought they were kidding. I haven't told my dad. He'll be bitter."

WING **MANNY LEGACE**, ON DISCOVERING HIS NAME HAD BEEN MISSPELLED ON THE STANLEY CUP; IT WAS LATER CORRECTED

"Luc Robitaille is a great kid and a good player, but ask anybody on the street and they'd probably think Luc Robitaille is a type of salad dressing."

KINGS OWNER **BRUCE McNALL**, ON WHY HE HAD TO BRING WAYNE GRETZKY TO LOS ANGELES IN 1988

"Holezig, Kulzig, what's his name is no Terry Sawchuck."

BRUINS GM **HARRY SINDEN**, ON CAPITALS GOALIE OLAF KOLZIG, JUST BEFORE LOSING A PLAYOFF SERIES TO WASHINGTON

"I was never going to be a player to get standing ovations in a visitor's building. I realized from Day One, the way I played, I'd never be a Gretzky or a Lemieux. Well, a Mario, I mean."

AVALANCHE **CLAUDE LEMIEUX**, ON GETTING USED TO BEING HATED BY OPPOSING PLAYERS AND FANS

"Not a nice story. Brian Sutter said I looked like Charles Manson. He called me Charlie, then it became Killer."

CANADIEN **DOUG GILMOUR**, ON THE SOURCE OF HIS "KILLER" NICKNAME

"Being called a frog 20 times a day is something that ends up getting on your nerves."

WING **MARTIN LAPOINTE**, ON AN ARGUMENT AND FIGHT HE HAD WITH HIS TEAM CANADA TEAMMATE ERIC LINDROS BEFORE THE 1991 JUNIOR WORLD CHAMPIONSHIP

"I tell people this all the time, whether it's the Stanley Cup or a bantam triple-A championship or the gold medal, you've got to line up the moon and the stars to win it. It doesn't just happen."

TEAM CANADA COACH **MIKE BABCOCK**, ON THE FINE LINE BETWEEN WINNING AND LOSING

"If you play well and win you're a heck of a leader; you don't win you're an okay leader, and if you don't play well and you don't win, you're a lousy leader."

WINGS CAPTAIN **STEVE YZERMAN**

"When your goalie is sharp, you have a chance to win every game. If he's not, you don't have a chance to win any game."

BLACKHAWKS COACH **BRIAN SUTTER**

"Winning is always fun, but the car is more important.""

DUCK **TEEMU SELANNE**, ON THE ALL-STAR GAME MVP AWARD

"I score most of my goals in the third period because I don't like to lose."

ISLANDER MARK PARRISH

Winning **does**